Send Your Spirit

Send Your Spirit

Prayers for Parents of Teenagers

Carl Koch

Saint Mary's Press
Christian Brothers Publications
Winona, Minnesota

The publishing team included Michael Wilt, development editor; Rebecca Fairbank, copy editor; James H. Gurley, production editor; Zach Marrel, cover designer; pre-press, printing, and binding by the graphics division of Saint Mary's Press.

The acknowledgments continue on page 152.

Printed in the United States of America

Printing: 9 8 7 6 5 4 3 2 1

Year: 2007 06 05 04 03 02 01 00 99

ISBN 0-88489-568-8

For my godchildren—
Sam, Simon, Kevin, and Ryan—
and their parents

Contents

Introduction

Then Jesus told them a parable about their need to pray always and not to lose heart. (Luke 18:1)

Persevere in prayer. (Romans 12:12)

Pray in the Spirit at all times in every prayer and supplication. To that end keep alert and always persevere in supplication. (Ephesians 6:18)

This sound advice from the Scriptures applies particularly to youth ministers, teachers, parents of teenagers, indeed, anyone who cares for teens. Sometimes prayer is the best and only help that we can offer teens. God always listens, cares, and offers grace.

The prayers in this book will prove useful to anyone who wants to nurture the growth and development of teenagers. They supply words when our own may seem insufficient or incoherent. In addition, these prayers touch on the key themes and issues in teenage life. Each prayer can be easily adapted to various situations.

One important feature of the prayers is that each includes a passage from the Bible. By including biblical passages, the prayers not only set our attention on God but also offer God's word to inspire, challenge, and comfort us. The prayers give us words with which to communicate with God and also provide us a way to listen to what God is telling us.

USING THESE PRAYERS

Before you offer a prayer, pause briefly using the Call to Presence at the beginning of the section to calm yourself and to bring to mind the teenager or teenagers about whom you wish to pray.

Read the selected prayer slowly, but naturally. Permit the words to sink in. Listen to the Scripture passage with your heart and mind open and welcoming.

Where the letter N (or its possessive form, N's) appears, say the name or names of the teenager or teenagers for whom you are praying. This symbol (⌒) indicates a place to insert your own words about a particular person or situation.

After you have offered the prayer, you may wish to add a short prayer of your own that personalizes it even further. For instance, after a prayer of praise and thanksgiving, you might say something like, "Tonight, I thank you, God, especially for ⟶."

These prayers may serve you well as morning or evening prayers and as sources of reflection or meditation.

It is hoped that however you use these prayers they will help you draw closer to the teenagers in your life and to the God who is the source of all life, all goodness, all wisdom.

The Wisdom
We Need

Call to Presence

All-wise God, you are here, now, ready to
shed your light on me.

*(Take a few moments to recall the teenager or
teenagers on whom you wish to focus your prayer.
Reflect on the wisdom you see in them as well as
the wisdom they may need in life right now.)*

ASK GOD FOR WISDOM
James 1:5

The Apostle James tells us: "If any of you is lacking in wisdom, ask God, who gives to all generously and ungrudgingly, and it will be given you." That is good news indeed.

God, I ask for wisdom in dealing with N. Teens confuse me. Sometimes I wonder if I am coming or going. I know that this is often how they feel, too. And even though N does not always give signs of wanting my "wisdom," help me to speak it when it is needed. Right now I need your wisdom about ⌒.

DISCUSSION AND COUNSEL
Sirach 37:16

All-wise God, teenagers tend to want answers
(and the answer they want!) right *now*. I guess
I am not all that different sometimes. But the
Scriptures say,

> Discussion is the beginning of every
> work,
> and counsel precedes every
> undertaking.

In other words, look before leaping to an
answer.

I want this to be true for N and me.
Instead of discussing, we argue, or I make a
declaration, or N just tells me what's what.
Help me know how to discuss matters with
N so that our undertakings are *our* undertakings, and counsel is really counsel. I
specifically could use your wisdom about
⁓.

WISDOM AND UNDERSTANDING
Adapted from Ephesians 1:17–19

Living God, I make Paul's prayer my own:
"May the God of Jesus our Savior give us
wisdom and understanding of all that has
been revealed. May we marvel at God's work
and see the hope that God offers us. The
inheritance God grants to us is rich. Great is
the power of our God."

I ask for wisdom and understanding,
particularly about N. Your power is great,
my God. Amen.

FALSE PROPHETS
Matthew 7:15–16

Merciful God, knowing the truth proves
difficult because we are surrounded by half-
truths and untruths from TV, advertisements,
people trying to put a spin on something for
their own benefit. Promises both false and
true tempt us in all directions. I cannot
always tell what's true, so it is no wonder
that N sometimes gets twisted around.

Jesus said, "Beware of false prophets,
who come to you in sheep's clothing but
inwardly are ravenous wolves. You will know
them by their fruits." Help me be aware of
false prophets, con artists, and cheats, and
help N, too. I am especially concerned that
N is being fooled by ⌒. Guide N in
dealing with this, and guide me in helping.

FERTILE GROUND FOR GOD'S WORD
Matthew 13:31–32

God's Reign is "like a mustard seed that someone took and sowed in his field; it is the smallest of all the seeds, but when it has grown it is the greatest of shrubs and becomes a tree, so that the birds of the air come and make nests in its branches."

God, may I be fertile ground that welcomes your Word in my soul so that your way grows in me. May I have the rich generosity of the tree that gives itself for the good of others—for their shade, for their shelter, for their nourishment. I especially need your Word rooted in my soul so that I can share it with N.

Truth That Sets Us Free
John 8:31–32

Jesus assured us: "If you continue in my word, you are truly my disciples; and you will know the truth, and the truth will make you free."

God, I desire the truth that will set me free—free from my compulsions, free from my anger and sadness, free from ignorance and division. With truth in my heart, grant me the strength to help set free N. May your words become a home for me, and for N. Open our eyes and ears, hearts and minds.

Do Not Be Conformed
Romans 12:2

Holy One, help me heed Paul's warning,
when he said, "Do not be conformed to this
world, but be transformed by the renewing of
your minds, so that you may discern what is
the will of God—what is good and accept-
able."

May I renew my mind through prayer,
through listening to your word, and by loving
my neighbors as myself. Then I can give ℵ
the kind of example that will lead to goodness. If I conform to the distorted values of
this world, I can hardly expect ℵ to conform
to your standards. God, renew and transform
me. I want to do your will. Show me what it
is, so that I can do good and grow in your
image.

RIGHT JUDGMENT
John 7:24

Jesus says, "Do not judge by appearances, but judge with right judgment."

Making up my mind on *N*'s outward appearance can be all too easy. When I take the easy way, I don't have to search for the heart of the matter or for what is really true. But true wisdom is not so easy, for it seeks to know the whole story.

God, send your Spirit into my heart and mind so that I may find out the truth and judge accordingly. Make me a seeker of truth. In particular, help me to see the truth of this situation ⌒ with *N*. Lead me, my God.

A Humble Heart
Proverbs 11:2–3

The Scriptures say,

> wisdom is with the humble.
> The integrity of the upright guides them.

God of all truth, grant me the wisdom of humility: that is, help me to learn from everyone and to listen to truth wherever it may be found, even from N. The humble recognize that everyone has some of your divine light shining out to the rest of us. None of us has all the answers to life's questions. Give me a humble heart so that I may attain the wisdom that will guide me with integrity.

For N I pray for wisdom and humility, too; may N have integrity as a constant guide.

WISDOM AND UNDERSTANDING
Proverbs 19:8

Holy One, I need wisdom and understanding if I am to be a source of wisdom and understanding for N. This is what you will for us. As the Scriptures make clear,

> To get wisdom is to love oneself;
>> to keep understanding is to prosper.

Pour forth your Spirit into me, Holy One, so that I keep my eyes, ears, and heart open to your wisdom wherever it may be found. Urge N and me to "keep understanding," to keep learning, to attend to your presence in our experiences and in our neighbors. In this way, Creator of us all, we will not only gain wisdom but we will love ourselves as well.

QUIET WORDS OF THE WISE
Ecclesiastes 9:16–18

Merciful God, I pray for wisdom, recalling
the words from the Scriptures that

> wisdom is better than might. . . .
> The quiet words of the wise are more to
> > be heeded
> > than the shouting of a ruler among
> > fools.
> Wisdom is better than the weapons of
> > war.

Indeed, without wisdom, we resort to
might and weapons of war. When N and I
interact, may we seek wisdom together rather
than power over each other. I cannot expect
N to be a seeker of wisdom if I am not. Help
me become a wise person with quiet words of
truth. Help us both become seekers of your
wisdom.

Discernment
Job 11:6

God, source of all wisdom, the Scriptures tell us that "wisdom is many-sided." All too often I seek and offer simple answers to complex questions. Teenagers need more than this. After all, your wisdom teaches us that most issues have many sides.

Help me be dissatisfied with oversimplification, with pat answers, with snap judgments. Lead me instead to stay with my discernment so that I see issues in all their facets, especially issues dealing with א. Give me steadfastness until your light breaks through my confusion.

Listening
and Waiting
with Patience

Call to Presence

Loving God, present here, you wait patiently for us to respond to your grace, and you listen to our every concern.

(Take a few moments to recall the teenager or teenagers on whom you wish to focus your prayer. For what do they yearn and need more patience? How might you be a model of listening and waiting?)

LISTEN
Psalm 34:11–13

God, you want us to listen carefully to one
another but also to speak the truth. As the
psalmist says,

> Come, sons and daughters, listen to me;
> I will teach you reverence for
>   Yahweh. . . .
> Keep your tongue from evil
> and your lips from speaking deceit.

We can hear the voice of God in the
wisdom of other people, including our
teenagers, but we must listen. In turn, God
directs us to speak honestly and to refrain
from words that hurt and manipulate. May
we listen and speak to our teenagers as God
would want us to. This is the way of true
wisdom, the wisdom we want to share.

BE ATTENTIVE
Exodus 23:20–21

God, you told the people of Israel in Exodus:
"I am going to send an angel in front of you,
to guard you on the way and to bring you to
the place that I have prepared. Be attentive
. . . and listen to [the angel's] voice."

    I am no angel, Holy One, but you do call
me to bring others to the place you have
prepared for us—your reign of justice, love,
and peace. So grant N and me the graces we
need to be attentive to each other and to your
Spirit present in each other. May we listen to
each other with the same respect that the
people of Israel gave to your messenger. I
particularly have a hard time listening to N
about ——. Help us improve our communication about this, and about all things.

MEMBERS OF ONE ANOTHER
Ephesians 4:25–26

God of mercy and compassion, you always listen to your people. Now I seek the graces that I need to do as Paul urges: "Putting away falsehood, let all of us speak the truth to our neighbors, for we are members of one another. Be angry but do not sin; do not let the sun go down on your anger."

Source of all truth, help me listen and speak the truth with N, remembering that we are part of the Body of Christ. And if we do grow angry with each other, help us forgive instead of turning to sarcasm, sniping, hateful words, or worse. May I always keep before me as a prayer, "we are members of one another." It would be a gift if N could remember this, too.

LISTEN AND ATTEND
Sirach 6:33

Your words are truth and life, Holy Wisdom.
So the Book of Sirach tells us,

> If you love to listen you will gain
>   knowledge,
>   and if you pay attention you will
>   become wise.

Help me learn to listen attentively, Source
of all wisdom, particularly during times
when listening to Ɲ is a challenge for me.
Help Ɲ likewise, especially when Ɲ does
not have an easy time listening to me. May
we remember these words from the Scriptures so that when we listen we learn, and
when we pay attention to each other we plant
the seeds of wisdom. God, help us listen and
attend.

TELLING STORIES
Matthew 13:13

Jesus explained to his disciples, "The reason I speak to them in parables is that 'seeing they do not perceive, and hearing they do not listen, nor do they understand.'"

Loving God, when I am speaking with N, may I choose words and stories that we both understand. May we communicate clearly so that we can both be wiser and better. Jesus taught us to tell stories, so strengthen us to share our stories and our experiences. Help me always remember that N has stories to tell, and give me ears and heart to hear them. Give N ears and heart to hear my tales, too.

CLARITY AND HUMILITY
Sirach 5:11–14

When I listen and speak, eternal God, may I be steady and strong in goodness. As the Scriptures say,

> Be quick to hear,
>> but deliberate in answering.
> If you know what to say, answer your
>> neighbor. . . .
> Do not be called double-tongued
>> and do not lay traps with your
>> tongue.

First, Holy One, help me listen carefully. Then, when I speak, may I be clear and honest; but when I have nothing to contribute, help me have the humility to hold my tongue. Come, aid us with the gifts of listening and speaking. I especially need your grace to listen when $\bigwedge$ speaks about ⌁. Guide me, God.

Patience and Love
1 Corinthians 13:4

God, you are love, and you command us to love. This is your central commandment, which leads to good life. You know that I love N. But I need patience, the patience that Paul talks about when he says, "Love is patient; love is kind."

It's not surprising that the first quality Paul attributes to love is patience. When N does this ‿, I get impatient. And I know when I do this ‿, N gets impatient. And our impatience strains and injures our love. So, patient God, give us both this key virtue so that we may continue, through patience, to grow in our love for each other.

Patience in Teaching
2 Timothy 4:1–2

God of all goodness, as an adult, I am called to be a teacher to younger people. When I was young, an adult's impatience did me no good. I got defensive, angry, maybe even scared. Help me keep the words of Timothy before me: "I solemnly urge you: proclaim the message . . . with the utmost patience in teaching."

God, help me to patiently impart my knowledge to *N*, to gear my expectations to *N*'s needs and abilities at a given time. In this way may I be a witness to your love for *N*. Divine and patient Teacher, hear my prayer.

PATIENCE AND GROWTH
James 5:7–8

Open my heart, eternal God, to hear these words from the Scriptures: "Be patient, therefore, beloved, until the coming of the Lord. The farmer waits for the precious crop from the earth, being patient with it until it receives the early and the late rains. You also must be patient."

I do get impatient; I would be lying if I claimed otherwise. Teenagers can be maddening. I want N to grow up sooner rather than later, but like the farmer's crops, people grow in their own time. Grant me patience with N, and grant N patience with self, others, and life.

PATIENT AND CALM
Sirach 1:23–24

God, may I always heed the advice of Sirach:

> Those who are patient stay calm until the
> right moment,
> and then cheerfulness comes back to
> them.
> They hold back their words until the
> right moment.

If I can learn to listen for the right moment
in patience, I will come a long way toward
communicating well with N.

Grant me the graces of patience, cheerful-
ness, and good timing, particularly in dealing
with N. May N be patient with me, too. I
am not patient enough to stay calm yet, but
with your grace, my God, it can be so.

Steadfast Love

Call to Presence

God, you are love, present with me now.

(Take a few moments to recall the teenager or teenagers on whom you wish to focus your prayer. In what ways do they need to know your love? How can you be loving with them?)

BANDS OF LOVE
Hosea 11:4

Loving God, all through history you have
forgiven our evil ways and led us back to
you. To your lost people, you declared:

> I led them with cords of human kindness,
>   with bands of love.

Give me a kind and forgiving heart so
that I may love אּ in times of depression,
loneliness, despair, and confusion. May I be
your "bands of love." God of all goodness,
may I never forget that you constantly forgive
us and invite us to love. From my love, may
אּ learn kindness, charity, and love.

"I HAVE CALLED YOU FRIENDS"
John 15:12–15

God, you brought us into a new and intimate relationship with you through Jesus. He tells us, "This is my commandment, that you love one another as I have loved you. . . . I do not call you servants any longer . . . I have called you friends."

Well, God, all of us are commonplace, frail, ordinary humans. Help me treat N as I would treat Jesus. Let me love N with all the kindness, respect, and generosity that I would offer to Christ. As time passes and as N matures, let us be true friends of each other just as Jesus is a true friend to me.

Good Works
Acts of the Apostles 9:36

God of love, you created us to love. All the
Apostles and holy women and men throughout history have known this. When Jesus or
the disciples wanted to praise someone, they
pointed to their charity. In the Acts of the
Apostles, one such holy woman is introduced
in this way: "In Joppa there was a disciple
whose name was Tabitha. . . . She was
devoted to good works and acts of charity."

God, give me the grace to love ℵ and to
do good works and acts of love for people in
need, so that when I come to the end of my
life I can look back and realize that I have not
wasted it. Love gives substance to my faith.
Help me, God, who is love, to be an example
of your love to ℵ. May ℵ then grow in
love, too.

Universal Love
1 Timothy 1:3–5

Creator of the universe, Jesus urged us to love universally, to love even our enemies. Paul tells Timothy: "I urge you . . . to remain in Ephesus so that you may instruct certain people. . . . The aim of such instruction is love that comes from a pure heart, a good conscience, and sincere faith."

God, send me grace that my love will be universal, inclusive of all my sisters and brothers, no matter their race, religion, ethnic background, no matter how they look, dress, or where they live. In particular, give me a pure heart, a good conscience, and sincere faith to love N. Let me put nothing in the way of love. I especially need grace to deal with N about ⌒. Guide me, God of love.

WHEN IT IS TOUGH TO LOVE
Luke 6:35

God, your call to love is not always simple or
easy, especially when Jesus said, "Love your
enemies, do good, and lend, expecting
nothing in return." It's one thing to love
others, especially teenagers, when they are
cooperative, interested, and listening well,
but quite another when they are surly,
argumentative, negative, or belligerent.

You promised us all the grace we would
need. So, God of all power, send me your
power that I may follow Jesus' command to
love, to do good, and to give, even when
times are hard and moods are harsh. Even
when it is tough to love, I know I can do so
with your grace. Send your powerful Spirit
upon N as well, that the love we give may
be returned in kind.

LOVING OTHERS,
LOVING GOD
1 John 4:20

God of truth, we cannot love you if we do
not love other people. As the Scriptures say,
"Those who say, 'I love God,' and hate their
brothers or sisters, are liars; for those who do
not love a brother or sister whom they have
seen, cannot love God whom they have not
seen." Once again you challenge me to be
consistent.

God, help me to remember your words
when I am tempted to spout angry words at
N, or to be manipulative, or to just turn N
off for the sake of my own mood or conve-
nience. In my heart I know I want to love N.
Send your help that I might do so, and teach
N to love, too.

LIFE-GIVING LOVE
1 John 3:14

The Apostle John declares, "We know that we
have passed from death to life because we
love one another. Whoever does not love
abides in death." God, I know this to be true.
Love gives life; hate kills.

Grant me the grace to care for, listen to,
and empathize with N, and especially to
guide N wisely. In loving N, both our lives
will be more full. By your grace may N
come to experience life filled with joy, hope,
creativity, and freedom from despair and
anger. Thank you, God, for strengthening our
ability to love.

Tongues of Angels
1 Corinthians 13:1

Love is the key to Christian and human life. Paul says, "If I speak in the tongues of mortals and of angels, but do not have love, I am a noisy gong or a clanging cymbal."

Love is the language we all wish to hear. May my words and acts of kindness, support, affirmation, and even challenge draw א and me to be our better selves, the selves you created us to be. May we speak with love in our heart and in our words so that we build up rather than tear down, bring peace and not war.

The Law of Love
Romans 13:8

Paul writes, "Owe no one anything, except to love one another; for the one who loves another has fulfilled the law." Sometimes this is no easy task during the bumpy roads of the teenage years. We know that learning to love and continuing to love take courage, faith, and hope. These virtues come from you alone, our God.

God, give N and me courage to get to know each other better all the time, to build trust between us, to hope that our care for each other will constantly grow. Thank you, our God, for giving us a law that tells us to love, and thank you for Jesus, who showed us how to love.

WELCOME ONE ANOTHER
Romans 15:7

Accepting N is not all that simple. Like
most teenagers—most people really—N
has some annoying habits and disagreeable
mannerisms. These sometimes make N hard
to accept.

But the Scriptures tell me, "Welcome one
another, therefore, just as Christ has wel-
comed you, for the glory of God." Well, God,
the only way this is possible is with your
grace. When I am fed up with N, and when
N is fed up with me, may we recall that you
always stand ready to welcome us, that you
accept us just as we are, and that you are
filled with the hope that we will love each
other in return.

LOVE IS THE FOCUS
1 Corinthians 13:2

Jesus made love the focal point of Christian life. As Paul says, "If I have prophetic powers, and understand all mysteries and all knowledge . . . but do not have love, I am nothing."

Without love we are nothing. Nothing— that's a very strong word. But we know this is true, of Paul, of N, of me, of all people. Love makes us somebody special, and when we give love we feel the power of God flowing through us. God, give N and me the power to love. Help us both to make love the center of our life and the focus of our energies. In this way may we help create the good life of your Reign.

LOVE IS . . .
1 Corinthians 13:4–7

Love is a tall order for anyone—a lifetime
goal learned slowly, with your grace, God
of love. "Love is patient; love is kind; love is
not envious or boastful or arrogant or rude.
It does not insist on its own way; it is not
irritable or resentful; it does not rejoice in
wrongdoing, but rejoices in the truth. It bears
all things, believes all things, hopes all things,
endures all things."

Sometimes Paul's description of love is
the opposite of my description of a teenager:
arrogant, rude, selfish, irritable, resentful, and
so on. Well, God, if N is to learn love from
me, then give me the grace to put on love
with all the qualities that Paul lists here. May
your grace fill N, too. I want love for N
because it is your way, the way of a life in
abundance.

Lasting Hope

Call to Presence

Gracious God, source of all hope, you are
present with us now and always.

*(Take a few moments to recall the teenager or
teenagers on whom you wish to focus your prayer.
How are they hopeful and not so hopeful? How do
you manifest hope to them?)*

ABOUND IN HOPE
Romans 15:13

When considering the lives of teenagers, we
need all the hope we can muster. Teenagers
are often the subject of talk about the hopelessness of their present and future. But who
are we to toss away hope?

Jesus was a person of hope, even though
he was constantly badgered by the authorities
and then crucified unjustly. Paul the Apostle
had hope, even though he was shipwrecked,
thrown into prison, lashed, and finally mur-
dered by his enemies. Paul wrote, "May the
God of hope fill you with all joy and peace in
believing, so that you may abound in hope by
the power of the Holy Spirit."

God of hope, grant me hope, especially
as it concerns N. May I trust that you are
leading N and me ultimately to you and
therefore to peace, joy, and the completion of
love.

Anchor of the Soul
Hebrews 6:19–20

With you our God, through Jesus the Christ, "we have this hope, a sure and steadfast anchor of the soul, a hope that enters the inner shrine behind the curtain, where Jesus, a forerunner on our behalf, has entered."

   I'm not sure that the anchor of hope is attached to my soul, my God, particularly where N is concerned. I want to be more hopeful. I want to hold fast to my hope in you so that I can have hope in N. My God, my redeemer, be with me. Fill me with hope so that I can be the kind of example that N needs. Come, Jesus, dwell in my soul, my inner shrine.

HOPE THROUGH TEARS
Luke 6:21

Gracious God, the beatitude

> Blessed are you who weep now,
> for you will laugh

gives me hope. Anyone who loves teenagers—loves anyone—will probably weep; I'm in that group. The teenage years are filled with changes, minor and major revolutions and revelations, challenges, blowups, anger, and tears. My experience with N confirms this time and time again.

Help me keep my head facing toward the horizon, even when tears cloud my vision. Guide me with hope that someday all will be well. Flood N with hope, too, so that we may both come to laughter and celebration. Plant hope in my heart, deep and firm, and I will know that your grace is with us.

Hold Fast to Hope
Hebrews 10:23

God, you give us reasons to hope—to see beyond the present with faith in your promise that all finally will be well. Over and over you proved that you are the source of hope. So, as Paul told the Hebrews, "Let us hold fast to the confession of our hope without wavering, for [Christ] who has promised is faithful."

Many disappointments about teenagers, including N, sometimes rob us of hope, but you promise to be with us in all our difficulties. I cling to this promise as the reason for hope. Strengthen me with hopefulness, particularly in regard to N. Faithful God, be with N and with me. Do not let us give in to despair.

SUSTAIN OUR HOPE
Adapted from Psalm 119:115–116

My God, "As you have promised, sustain us that we may live. Do not disappoint us in our hope." I have to hope in you, living God, because your wisdom is eternal, your promises to believers, true. Sustain my hope, in particular, as I deal with ᴎ.

I can live fully only if I act according to your light, so shine your light into my darkness and into the life of ᴎ. My efforts will always be disappointed if you, God, are not at the center of them. In my dealings with ᴎ, keep me focused on knowing and doing your will. In your light and presence, both ᴎ and I can go forward in hope. Sustain us that we may live.

SWEET WISDOM
Proverbs 24:13–14

Divine Teacher, one of your proverbs says:

> My child, eat honey, for it is good,
>> and the drippings of the honeycomb
>>> are sweet to your taste.
> Know that wisdom is such to your soul;
>> if you find it, you will find a future,
>> and your hope will not be cut off.

Send me such sweet wisdom so that I may keep my face toward the future and have rich hope. All wisdom comes from you, my God, and I certainly need it. Right now, fill me with the honey of your wisdom in dealing with N. Guide me in all things, God of hopeful wisdom.

WE STAND IN GRACE
Romans 5:1–2

Merciful God, Jesus came to offer us hope. His Resurrection from the dead conquered death once and for all. So Paul declared, "Therefore, since we are justified by faith, we have peace with God through our Lord Jesus Christ, through whom we have obtained access to this grace in which we stand; and we boast in our hope of sharing the glory of God."

We do stand in grace. May I never forget that. Especially now in coping with N, ground our hope in one fact: that all of us stand in your grace, all of us have a share in your glory. Teenagers and those of us who try to guide, nurture, and challenge them depend on your grace and our hope in sharing your glory. Come, Spirit of grace and hope, come to N and me.

CHARACTER AND HOPE
Romans 5:3–5

Paul tried to encourage the Romans with these words: "Suffering produces endurance, and endurance produces character, and character produces hope, and hope does not disappoint us, because God's love has been poured into our hearts through the Holy Spirit that has been given to us."

Caring for, loving, and leading $\mathcal{N}$ have caused me at times to suffer. You, God, must judge whether endurance has produced character and hope in me and in $\mathcal{N}$. Whatever the case, you will never disappoint us. Pour your love into our souls to increase our hope. Spirit of God, help us realize now and always that you are with us to guide us in the ways of hopeful living. I pray especially for hope with regard to $\mathcal{N}$.

TRUST GOD
Sirach 2:3–6

I need the hope that only you can give, God of all goodness. Help me remember your words in Sirach, in tough times but also in good times:

> Cling to [God], . . .
> > thus will your future be great.
> Accept whatever befalls you,
> > in crushing misfortune be patient;
> For in fire gold is tested,
> > and [the] worthy in the crucible of
> > > humiliation.
> Trust God and [God] will help you;
> > make straight your ways and hope in
> > > [God].

We could all do without the testing of misfortune, but we can have hope in you, our God. Help us now, particularly about ⁓. Guide us as we make straight our ways to you. I do cling to you, trustworthy God.

Hope in the Unseen
Romans 8:24–25

God, your servant Paul said: "Now hope that
is seen is not hope. For who hopes for what is
seen? But if we hope for what we do not see,
we wait for it with patience." This is a hard
truth. All the unknowns about what's going
to become of a young person we care about
stretch our ability to believe, to hope, and to
love.

Help me wait with patience and hope. I
seldom wait patiently or hopefully where N
is concerned. I desire only good for N. But
our relationship has its ups and downs. May I
not be overcome by the downs. In trials, give
me patience. In joy, give me gratitude. But
always keep the fragile seeds of hope for N
growing in my soul, until all things are made
new in you, our Creator.

Strengthening
Faith

Call to Presence

Faithful God, I acknowledge your caring presence with me now.

(Take a few moments to recall the teenager or teenagers on whom you wish to focus your prayer. What questions about faith seem to bother them? How is your faith clear to them?)

Grace of Faith
Hebrews 11:1

Healing God, in my relationship with ℵ.
I need to keep in my mind and heart these
words from the Letter to the Hebrews: "Faith
is the assurance of things hoped for, the
conviction of things not seen."

Send your grace of faith so that even
though we cannot know the future, both ℵ
and I may have hope that all will be well.
Give us the conviction that if we allow your
grace to work in us, we can do good and
make this world a more just, peaceful, and
charitable place. Send your faith to me and
to ℵ so that both of us may go forward in
hope.

PURE GIFT
Ephesians 2:8

Loving God, may I always remember that all life, all goodness, all truth come from you. Even faith is a pure gift. Paul says, "By grace you have been saved through faith, and this is not your own doing; it is the gift of God."

Thank you, God, for the gift of faith. Help N and me gain courage from the faith you give us. May we turn to you with our eyes steady and heart open. Faith is not something I can loan to N. It is a gift. But with your graceful guidance, I long to be an example of faith, a model of the gift, so that N may be more open to your gift, too.

GOD IS FAITHFUL
Psalm 145:13–14

Ever faithful God, may you lift up and
strengthen the faith in both N and me. As
the psalmist says:

> [God], you are faithful in all your words
> and holy in all your works.
> You lift up all who are falling
> and raise up all who are bowed down.

I certainly fall down, and troubles seem
to overwhelm me, so I understand what the
psalmist is saying. N falls and is bowed
down too sometimes. But you are faithful,
God, not only in words but in works. You
brought the Israelites out of slavery and sent
Jesus to save us from the bondage of death
and sin. Give N and me eyes to see your
faithful deeds in salvation history and in all
that is good and true and beautiful in our
world. May we set our heart on you, faithful
God. In particular I pray for N to have faith
in dealing with ⁓.

Do Not Be Afraid
Mark 6:50

Throughout Jesus' ministry he told people, "Take heart, it is I; do not be afraid." I certainly wish that I was not afraid of so many things and afraid for $\mathcal{N}$ so often. Faith is no easy proposition for me, and not for teenagers in general. Most of my fears for $\mathcal{N}$ are magnified because a teenager just does not have the experience to know that your grace, our God, will strengthen us, your words can guide us, and that ultimately you will prevail against the shadows of death and destruction.

God, give $\mathcal{N}$ and me the faith we need to take heart and be unafraid. Grant us the faith that you are with us because, in our fear, we are not always sure. Help $\mathcal{N}$ particularly to cope with and overcome fear of ⟶.

Faith and Works
James 2:26

God of mercy and compassion, open my
spirit and will to these challenging words
from the Scriptures: "For just as the body
without the spirit is dead, so faith without
works is also dead." Tough, radical words.

I cannot expect teenagers like N to
accept the blessings of faith if I do not demon-
strate my faith in deeds of justice, charity, and
peacemaking. Teenagers know that talk is
cheap, but actions have value. God, grace me
with the courage, sensitivity, and understanding I need to move my faith to works. I ask
that you move N to service of others, so
perhaps N's "works" will nurture faith, too.

ASK AND RECEIVE
Matthew 21:22

Holy One, open my heart and strengthen my spirit to hear these words of Jesus: "Whatever you ask for in prayer with faith, you will receive." As I read this, my God, I find it both an affirmation and a tremendous challenge. I am challenged to turn to you in prayer and then to believe that I will "receive" what I ask. It affirms my belief in your love.

The trouble I have with that passage, and I know teenagers question this a lot, is that I don't always receive what I ask for—at least as I understand my request. So I have to rely on my weak faith to believe that what happens is really what I asked for. That's a stretch of my faith for me, and it sure is for teens as well.

So grant N and me the grace to grow in faith. Then we will be able to move mountains—the mountains of our fears, our selfishness, our boredom, our timidity. Give us what we need, and help us understand the gift. Right now N may need faith, especially about ⌒ . Send us faith, Holy Friend.

THOSE WHO BRING GOOD NEWS
Romans 10:14–17

Holy One, may I be a bearer of the Good News to others, but particularly to ℵ. Strengthen and deepen my faith so that I can support and enlighten the faith of ℵ. May I always remember Paul's words to the Romans: "How are they to believe in one of whom they have never heard? And how are they to hear without someone to proclaim him? . . . As it is written, 'How beautiful are the feet of those who bring good news!' . . . So faith comes from what is heard, and what is heard comes through the word of Christ."

I have a hard time looking at my feet and seeing beauty, but the point is clear. I cannot expect ℵ to believe if I don't proclaim the Good News in my words, but more important, in the way I live. Clothe me, my God, in faith, hope, and effective love so that I may bring this word of Christ to ℵ and to all who hear me. Then ℵ can become a bearer of the Good News, too.

THE LIGHT OF GOD'S WORD
Psalm 119:105–108

O God,

> Your word is a lamp for my steps,
> a light to my path.
> I resolve and have taken an oath
> to follow your just decrees.
> I am sorely afflicted.
> Give me life according to your word.
> Accept the willing praise of my mouth,
>   O God,
> and teach me your decrees.

Surely, God, your word is a light to guide us. It is life-giving. Fill me with the light of your word because I need all the light I can find in order to be what I need to be for N. Inspire me to study your word, to pray and meditate on it, and to learn its wisdom and truth. In this way I can live in the fullness of your grace and be the kind of example that N needs. All praise and thanks to you for your holy word. For N, I ask that you teach "your decrees" about ⌒.

Sharing Faith
Philemon 1:4–6

God of compassion, fill me with faith so that
I may share my faith with N. Paul told his
friend Philemon: "I always thank my God
because I hear of your love for all the saints
and your faith toward the Lord Jesus. I pray
that the sharing of your faith may become
effective when you perceive all the good that
we may do for Christ."

My own faith toward Jesus has a fairly
shallow base, though I want it to take strong
root in my soul and grow large. For the sake
of N, I ask that my faith become more firm.
If my faith is weak, it won't mean a lot to N
when I share it. Fill me with faith, fill me with
faith.

GLORIOUS JOY
1 Peter 1:8–9

Gracious God, I pray for a more certain and steady faith in you and in Christ Jesus. Peter reminds us, "Even though you do not see [Christ] now, you believe in him and rejoice with an indescribable and glorious joy, for you are receiving the outcome of your faith, the salvation of your souls."

I do believe in Christ, but amid my fears, worries, doubts, and distractions, my faith is tested. The joy often escapes me. Send forth your grace, God, so that I may believe and experience the joy of firm faith. Send forth your grace, too, so that N may come to this same joy, and we will together be blessed by the salvation of our soul. At this moment N particularly needs your grace to cope with this challenge to belief: ⌒. Come, faithful God.

For the Many
Times Courage
Is Called For

Call to Presence

All-powerful and loving God, you dwell
within me. Hear my prayer.

*(Take a few moments to recall the teenager or
teenagers on whom you wish to focus your prayer.
In what situations do they need courage? What
support can you offer in these situations?)*

ABIDE WITH GOD
Adapted from 2 Chronicles 15:2–7

Spirit of God, open my senses, my heart,
and my will to hear your words spoken by
Azariah: "God is with you, when you abide
with God. Seeking, you will find God. . . .
While living godlessly, the times were
dangerous, chaotic, and confused. Peoples
fought with one another. So, you have
courage. Strengthen your heart and hand
because the Lord our God will reward your
efforts."

    Without your word guiding us and with-
out your power supporting us, N and I
cannot keep our integrity amid all the challenges and temptations that our world throws
at us. These times can be dangerous, chaotic,
and confusing for me, but even more so for
teenagers. So I call on you, God, once again
for light and strength. In a special way, N
needs courage in dealing with ⌒. Spirit
of God, be with us and fill us with courage.

TESTED IN FIRE
Adapted from Sirach 2:1–6

All-good God, courage comes from the
French word for "heart." So may we—*N*
and I—be of good and strong heart in all
things and recall your words:

> Those who serve God
>   must be ready to be tested.
> Set your heart in the right direction
>   and be strong.
> In times of disaster, do not weaken.
> Gold is always tested in fire.
> Trust God, and God will help you.
> Hold firm to the good and hope in God.

It is hard enough for me to have courage,
and teens now are tested in fires that I had
never heard of while growing up. Set our
heart in the right direction. Help us to hold
firm and be people of goodness and hope.
Specifically, I ask your courage for me in
dealing with ⸺. And I ask your courage
for *N* in dealing with ⸺.

Judgment and Understanding
Adapted from 1 Chronicles 22:11–13

The Book of Chronicles says: "God go with you so that you can successfully build God's place among humanity. May God give you good judgment and understanding. Have strength and courage."

God, with your help, we can be strong and courageous. We can make the earth a place where you reign. We can open our heart to you and become people of peace, justice, and virtue. God, you are with us today and every day. I ask especially that *N* be given good judgment and understanding, strength and courage. In a special way, guide and strengthen *N* in regard to ⸺.

SAFELY THROUGH THE STORM
Adapted from Acts of the Apostles 27:22–25

Being with a teenager is often like being on a ship in a storm. So, God, may Paul's words console me: "Take courage. An angel sent by God told me that God will bring us safely home. So don't be afraid. Be strong and have faith." Paul and the crew made it safely through the storm.

God, you never promised that life would be smooth sailing. But I know that you will bring us through life's storms if we have faith. Strengthen my faith and N's faith. With faith N can take heart and have courage in the face of discouragement, doubts, temptations, failures, and opposition. Bring N through the storms of teenage life just like you brought your Apostle Paul through the storm at sea. Bring me through the storms that come my way, too. Thank you, gracious God.

THE ARMOR OF GOD
Ephesians 6:10–11

"Be strong in the Lord and in the strength of [God's] power," Paul wrote. "Put on the whole armor of God." God, our protector, we—N and I—draw from your power and strength to gain the courage we need in our struggle with evil.

You, God, are courage and power. Indeed, only in you can we survive the temptations that surround us on every side: the temptations to greed, deceit, hatred, cheating, self-pity, and so on. Help us put on the armor that you give us with your grace: courage, kindness, honesty, patience, and selflessness. Then we can join you in fighting the good fight. As a teenager, N especially needs your armor to deal with ⌐‿⌐. May N be strong in your power.

GOD'S SUSTAINING PRESENCE
2 Chronicles 32:7–8

God, our strength, when N faces difficulties, let N remember the words your servant Hezekiah spoke: "Be strong and of good courage. Do not be afraid or dismayed. . . . With us is the Lord our God, to help us and to fight our battles." May N never forget your promise to always aid and assist us in any difficulty at hand. In particular, today N needs courage in this struggle ⌒.

I need your strength and courage to help N. May I always stay aware of your sustaining presence. May I make remembrance of you a constant part of my life. Guide me, give me courage, God of gods, Light of light.

DO NOT GROW WEARY
Galatians 6:2,7–9

Gracious God, may I be challenged and given courage by these words: "Bear one another's burdens, and in this way you will fulfill the law of Christ. . . . God is not mocked, for you reap whatever you sow. . . . So let us not grow weary in doing what is right, for we will reap at harvest time, if we do not give up."

I do grow weary of sowing good seeds that seem to be greeted with disagreement, disgust, or disdain. I sometimes get this feeling in my interactions with N. Even though I know that it is essential for teenagers to search, question, and even rebel, I do grow weary of it. Sometimes I want to give up. Give me the courage to act with charity, with perseverance and hope. And give N the courage to do what is right and to not give up.

WORDS OF TRUTH
Psalm 119:41–43

We pray with the psalmist:

> Let your steadfast love come to me,
>> O God,
>>> your salvation according to your
>>> promise.
> So shall I have an answer for those who
>> reproach me,
>>> for I trust in your words.
> Leave the word of truth in my mouth—
>> for in your decree is my hope.

Yes, steadfast God, leave your words of truth in our mouth and strengthen our will, so that the answer to difficulties is the example of our courage combined with charity. You are our hope; you make perseverance possible.

SALT AND LIGHT
Matthew 5:13–16

Just God, give N and me the courage to
follow the ultimate model of courage, Christ
Jesus. May we take to heart his words: "You
are the salt of the earth; but if salt has lost its
taste, how can its saltiness be restored? . . .
You are the light of the world. . . . Let your
light shine."

Keep me salty and filled with shining
light. May my salt give zest to all I do in your
name. May my light be a beacon of hope in
despair. In guiding and nurturing a teenager,
I need all the salt and light you can give me,
my God. And allow the salt and light in my
life to spill over to N and bless N's life
with zest, joy, hope, and goodness.

Wherever You Go
Joshua 1:5–9

God of all power, when Moses died, you did not desert our ancestors in faith. Your words to a fearful Joshua apply to me as well:

> As I was with Moses, so I will be with you; I will not fail you or forsake you. . . . Only be strong and very courageous, being careful to act in accordance with all the law that my servant Moses commanded you. . . . Be strong and courageous; do not be frightened or dismayed, for the LORD your God is with you wherever you go.

Be with ℵ and me wherever we go, God of power. In our relationship may we work together for good. Guide and strengthen us just as you did Joshua. With your help and in your presence, may I lead ℵ to the promise of your Reign. Teach us both your law and give us courage in the face of all that may scare or confuse us. May your presence with us be obvious and clear.

DANGEROUS TIMES
Adapted from 2 Chronicles 15:1–7

Spirit of God, may I hear in my heart your
words spoken by Azariah: "God is with you,
when you abide with God. Seeking, you will
find God. . . . While living godlessly, the
times were dangerous, chaotic, and confused.
Peoples fought with one another. So, you
have courage. Strengthen your heart and
hand because the Lord our God will reward
your efforts."

God of truth and power, I know that I
cannot sustain the courage I need to live the
good life without your word guiding me and
without your power supporting me—and
neither can Ν. These times can be dangerous, chaotic, and confusing. So I call on you,
God, once again for light and strength. Ν
particularly needs your courage, God, in
handling this ⸺. Abide with Ν and me
always. Thanks and praise to you, Holy
Friend.

Forgiving

Call to Presence

God of merciful forgiveness, be with me now
as I pray.

*(Take a few moments to recall the teenager or
teenagers on whom you wish to focus your prayer.
Where do they stand on the needs to forgive and be
forgiven? Where do you stand?)*

AMBASSADORS FOR CHRIST
2 Corinthians 5:18–20

Merciful God, help me always to remember that you call us to be reconcilers. This applies to my relationship with N as well as to my relationships with others. Paul told the divided people of Corinth: "God . . . has given us the ministry of reconciliation, . . . entrusting the message of reconciliation to us. So we are ambassadors for Christ."

Life with teenagers can be filled with conflict, tensions, disagreements, and hurts. God, may I be filled with the desire to seek reconciliation when I am at odds with N. May I never forget that as an adult I need to be a model of forgiveness and reconciliation. This is hard to do, so help me, merciful God.

GOD STANDS READY TO FORGIVE
Adapted from Nehemiah 9:17

Forgiving God, even when Israel continually wandered from the ways of righteousness, you forgave them. As Nehemiah says, "You, God, stand ready to forgive. You are gracious and faithful, and bountiful in love. You never abandoned sinful Israel."

God of mercy, help me forgive ℵ and myself readily and gladly. May I be as courteous, gracious, and trustworthy as you have always been. God, never abandon me to anger and grudges and the destruction they cause. Rather, plant in my heart your forgiving, generous Spirit.

Burdened with Sin
Adapted from Psalm 65:2–3

All of us sin. Virtue alludes us. As the psalmist says: "All flesh comes to God burdened with sin, overwhelmed with failings. Even so, God pardons human shortcomings."

God, we do wrong in a million ways, some small and some large. We tell small fibs and big lies. We spread rumors and even slander. We ignore those who are hungry, and we pollute the earth. Help me admit my sins and open my heart to your grace, grace I need to turn back to your way, your truth, your life. And, realizing my own need for forgiveness, may I be forgiving of the faults of N.

GOOD FROM EVIL
Adapted from Genesis 50:19–20

In the Book of Genesis, Joseph forgave his brothers even though they had sold him into slavery. He reassured them: "Don't be afraid of me. You did me a great harm, but God has brought good from it."

God, you can always bring good from evil. One of the greatest evils is having a hard heart toward those who have done us wrong. By forgiving, we too can see what good can come from a bad situation. Lead me to have a forgiving spirit and a wider perspective so that I can see and do good, especially where $\mathcal{N}$ is concerned. May I freely forgive this ⌐⌐⌐. Then, like Joseph, I can say, "Don't be afraid," and no one will need to be.

DO NOT JUDGE
Luke 6:37

Jesus taught his followers: "Do not judge, and you will not be judged; do not condemn, and you will not be condemned. Forgive, and you will be forgiven."

Merciful God, I find it easy to judge other people without trying to understand them. Then I pass sentence. Meanwhile, I hate to be judged. God, open my heart and mind to N. Help me to not judge and condemn but to listen and put aside my anger so that I can understand N better. And may I readily forgive, just as you forgive me. It is not easy, but with your grace it is possible. And may N forgive me, too.

As We Forgive Those . . .
Adapted from Luke 11:4

The Lord's Prayer asks God to "forgive us our trespasses, as we forgive those who trespass against us."

Living God, how often are we really honest when we pray that line? Surely we want your forgiveness, but do we really forgive those who have betrayed our trust or done us other harm? Maybe we do sometimes, but more often we probably don't forgive. Something in us wants what we think of as our rights. God, shower me with your grace so that when I say, "as we forgive those who trespass against us," I am speaking from the heart and not just mouthing pious words.

I need this grace particularly with $\mathcal{N}$ about ⌒.

FORGIVE AGAIN AND AGAIN
Adapted from Luke 17:3–4

God of mercy, Jesus gave us some hard commands. Here is one that we find especially difficult: "If people sin, counsel them to reform. If the sinners change, forgive them. Even if they sin against you seven times every day, but repent each time, you must forgive them."

God, that's asking a lot of me. So much in our culture tells us just the opposite: "Don't get mad, get even"; "Fool me once, shame on you; fool me twice, shame on me." Instead, faithful God, teach N and me how to follow the counsel of your Son, to reform our ways so that we may forgive each other. N and I cannot learn such forgiveness without you, our God. In particular, I need your grace to forgive N about ⁓.

FATHER, FORGIVE THEM
Luke 23:34

From his cross, Jesus cried out, "Father, forgive them; for they do not know what they are doing." He asked your forgiveness, God, for all the people who wanted to see him suffer and die a long and torturous death.

We excuse ourselves when we need forgiveness by claiming that we didn't know what we were doing. On the other hand, we all too often balk at giving teenagers the benefit of the doubt. God, give me the heart and will of your Son, Jesus, who forgave his persecutors even as he neared his last breath. Help me to be forgiving. In the heat of difficult moments, may I remember Jesus. I need this reminder, especially in dealing with N about ⁓. Help me, gracious God.

TOLERANCE
Colossians 3:13

Paul said to the Colossians, "Bear with one another and, if anyone has a complaint against another, forgive each other; just as the Lord has forgiven you, so you also must forgive."

In all honesty, all-good God, N and I would probably offend each other less if we could "bear with one another," if we had more tolerance. Grant both of us the grace to be tolerant. Then, if we still argue, help us to forgive. We are not you, God, but you give us the grace to imitate your ability to forgive. Be with N and me, forgiving God, as we forgive one another.

FORGIVE ONE ANOTHER
Adapted from Sirach 28:2

Merciful God, you promise pardon of our sins
when we forgive others. Sirach says: "Pardon
your neighbors when they do you harm. As a
result, your own sins will be forgiven when
you come to prayer. If you hoard anger
against other people, how can you expect
healing from God?"

That salty, wise character Huckleberry
Finn declared that we cannot pray a lie. Well,
gracious God, that applies here, too. I can
hardly pray for your forgiveness if I have no
forgiveness for N. Healing comes when we
forgive. So, God, teach us to forgive each
other and give us the courage and compassion to do so, especially in dealing with
⟶.

BEFORE THE SETTING OF THE SUN
Adapted from Ephesians 4:26,32

Paul told the community at Ephesus, "You will sometimes be angry. That's reality, but do not let your anger spill over into sin. Do not let the sun set on your anger. . . . Rather, be kind to one another and forgiving."

God, you inspired Paul to give this wise advice. If we do not seek to forgive and put aside our anger, it causes us no end of sleeplessness. We brood, and our anger just grows. Instead of that, help Ν and me to deal with conflict right away, to do what we can to settle matters peacefully, to forgive and get on with living before the setting of the sun. Come, Spirit of God, give both of us a heart of kindness, forgiveness, and peace. I need this forgiving heart, particularly with Ν about ⌒.

Making Peace
Colossians 1:20

Saving God, you sent Jesus to bring us back into harmony with you and with one another. As the Scriptures say, "Through him God was pleased to reconcile . . . all things, whether on earth or in heaven, by making peace."

You send us into the world to follow in the footsteps of Jesus. We are called to be peacemakers for the good of all the world. An obvious place for me to start is with Ν. My attempts at making peace with Ν are pleasing in your sight. Help me take up the banner of peace by always striving to speak words of peace, harmony, and joy to Ν. In a specific way, help us to make peace with one another over this ⁓.

Rites of Passage

Call to Presence

Living God, I remember that you are with me now and always.

(Take a few moments to recall the teenager or teenagers on whom you wish to focus your prayer. Ponder the rite or rites of passage they are involved in right now. What are your feelings and hopes for them?)

STARTING TO DATE
Proverbs 24:13–14

Gracious God, one of your proverbs says:

> My child, eat honey, for it is good,
> > and the drippings of the honeycomb
> > > are sweet to your taste.
> Know that wisdom is such to your soul;
> > if you find it, you will find a future,
> > and your hope will not be cut off.

Send such sweet wisdom to N, who now embarks on the adventure of dating. It should be a sweet experience, but it can be so difficult, too. Give N the wisdom to enjoy building good relationships without getting caught up in unrealistic expectations. Guide me in offering helpful counsel and useful support. I know that all wisdom comes from you, our God, and N and I certainly need it. Guide us in all things, God of hopeful wisdom.

First Job
Galatians 6:4–5

God, part of growing up is learning to work for a living. Please help N see work as part of cocreating, with you, a better world. Saint Paul wrote, "All must test their own work; then that work, rather than their neighbor's work, will become a cause for pride. For all must carry their own loads."

In this first job, God, be present as N carries a new load. Help N take pride in a job truly well done. In the process help N to work responsibly—conscientiously, carefully, diligently, and cheerfully. Give N perseverance, courage, and optimism in the face of new tasks and responsibilities.

LEARNING TO DRIVE
Ephesians 5:15–18

God of the journey, Ν is on the road, driv-ing! Though I know what a big deal it is, Ν's driving scares the wits out of me. I fret and stew, wondering if I will get a call from the state patrol. I pray that Ν will somehow do as Paul said: "Be careful then how you live, not as unwise people but as wise, mak-ing the most of the time. . . . Do not be foolish. . . . Do not get drunk."

Having been a teen myself, and knowing how I drove, I worry that Ν will be careless and make foolish mistakes. Good Shepherd, protect and guide Ν and all other drivers, young and old, and lead them back home. At the same time, soothe my fears.

TRYING OUT OR AUDITIONING
2 Timothy 1:6–7

My Creator, N is trying out for ⁓.
Success or failure will determine if this is to
be a joyful or a painful experience. Either
way, help N to do their best and to accept
gracefully the responsibilities that come with
success, or the learning and growth that
accompany failure.

In all ways, and especially regarding this
particular interest, help me encourage N.
It is important for us to nurture our gifts,
whatever they may be, and to help our loved
ones nurture their gifts as well. As the
Scriptures say, "Rekindle the gift of God that
is within you . . . for God did not give us a
spirit of cowardice, but rather a spirit of
power and of love and of self-discipline."

God, I pray for all these gifts for N.
Grant N courage, power, love, and self-
discipline—important gifts, whether success
or failure results. Grant me these gifts, too, so
that I can be a source of strong support and
sensitive encouragement.

FIRST BREAKUP
Psalm 77:1–2,11

Breaking up the first time, dear God, is
terrible for a teen—it's hard enough even
after we've done it several times. God, please
somehow remind N that all your children,
N included, are always loved and lovable.
Break through any gloom and self-doubt with
your rays of sunshine and hope.

Help me to be with N with compassion,
listening, and calm support. Right now, I pray
for N with the words of the psalmist:

> I cried aloud to you, O God;
>> I cried, and you heard me.
> In the day of my distress I sought you,
>>> Yahweh,
>>> and by night I stretched out my
>>> hands in prayer. . . .
> Then I remember your deeds;
>> I recall your wonders in times gone
>> by.

May N remember all the good gifts in life,
and avoid dwelling on negative thinking and
a sense of hopelessness. Help set N's eyes
on the future.

A Friend Moves Away
Isaiah 49:15–16

Living God, it is almost inevitable that we
will go through the experience of having a
friend move away. It has happened to me,
and it is now happening to N. Such a loss is
a time for grieving, and it is a rite of passage
as well: N now needs to regroup and
somehow move on.

Be with N amid this period of sadness
and grieving. May N's other friends and me
help to make N feel less alone. Especially,
show your constant love for N, the kind of
love you described in Isaiah when you said:

> Can a woman forget her nursing child,
> > or show no compassion for the child
> > > of her womb?
> Even these may forget,
> > yet I will not forget you.
> See, I have inscribed you on the palms of
> > my hands.

Hold N in the palm of your hand during
this tough time, this time of change.

Searching
for the Next Step
1 Peter 4:10

Good and kind Creator, N is at the point
where a life decision must be made. Graduation nears, admissions deadlines come close,
pressure for making some choices mounts. I
know and you know, and N knows, that
many decisions made today may be changed
tomorrow. Nevertheless, N has to take some
steps for the future.

Grant N and me the graces we need to
discern what is best, what steps will make the
best use of N's gifts—that is really what is
most important. Peter reminds us: "Like good
stewards of the manifold grace of God, serve
one another with whatever gift each of you
has received." As N and I sort through
these next steps, keep these gifts clearly
before us so we may discern how they might
be best used for the good of all.

A Major Success
Sirach 10:5,12

Praise and thanks to you, good and gracious God, for the major success in the life of Ɲ. We all need such successes to lift our spirit and remind us of the many gifts you have given us. So I celebrate this success of Ɲ and thank you, God.

I also pray that Ɲ will remember that you, God, are the source of all good things. May Ɲ and I recall these words of Sirach:

> Human success is in the hand of the Lord,
>   and it is [God] who confers
>   honor. . . .
> The beginning of human pride is to
>   forsake the Lord.

So, may both of us always turn to you in prayer: for wisdom to guide us in what is true and right, for courage to follow your ways, and in rejoicing when success is the end result.

A Major Failure
Romans 5:3–5

Merciful God, N has just experienced a major failure. I know and N knows that failure is part of life, but such recognition does not soothe our sufferings when we actually do fail. This failure bruises N's self-confidence and stands as a sign of a goal unachieved, something left undone.

Help me help N cope with this failure. It has been said that in strictly human terms, Jesus failed, dramatically and tragically, in his mission. Many other people we consider "successes" experienced profound failures on their way to success. Guide me to help N take consolation and challenge from Paul's words to the Romans: "We also boast in our sufferings, knowing that suffering produces endurance, and endurance produces character, and character produces hope, and hope does not disappoint us, because God's love has been poured into our hearts." May this failure urge N onward, adding strength to character and leading to new hope.

FACING SEXUAL BOUNDARIES
1 Corinthians 6:19–20

Creator, you shaped us as sexual beings.
Sexuality is a wonderful part of our life; its
energy draws us into relationships and
communion with others. For teens, it is also
a source of enormous confusion and terrible
tension.

Today I pray for N, who faces decisions
about sexual boundaries and is trying to deal
with all the pressures teens are under to ex-
press their sexuality through sexual activity.
May I help in ways that are wise, empathetic,
and effective. Most of all, may N remember
these words from the Scriptures: "Your body
is a temple of the Holy Spirit within you,
which you have from God. . . . You are not
your own. . . . Therefore glorify God in
your body." Holy One, may N sense your
sacred presence within and make decisions
that will indeed glorify you.

DEATH OF A
SIGNIFICANT PERSON
1 Thessalonians 4:13–18

Living God, N has just experienced the loss
of ⁀, someone very significant. I know
that N will grieve, and that is only right.
Loss of a significant person is a painful rite of
passage, one that causes us to question many
things, including your role in the loss and
even your existence.

God, grant both N and me a lively faith
and a firm hope that those who have died
abide with you in love. May N not cling to
grief for long, but come to a point of acceptance, letting go, and healing. Let these words
from the Scriptures form a strong support in
N's grieving: "We do not want you to be
uninformed, brothers and sisters, about those
who have died, so that you may not grieve as
others do who have no hope. For since we
believe that Jesus died and rose again, even
so, through Jesus, God will bring with him
those who have died. . . . Therefore encourage one another with these words." I do
believe in resurrection with Jesus; please,
deepen my faith and the faith of N.

GRADUATION
1 Timothy 6:18–19

Holy Friend, N graduates soon. I am not
sure that either of us is ready for this step.
Such transitions hit us with joy and sadness,
hope and regret, relief and anxiety, and endless questions about the future. Nevertheless,
I give you thanks for bringing N to this
moment of accomplishment.

You have created us all for good. Having
reached this point, may N not worry so
much about the future but see it as the next
opportunity for adventure and service. May
N have the grace that Paul wanted for the
community he advised "to do good, to be rich
in good works, generous, and ready to share,
thus storing up for themselves the treasure of
a good foundation for the future, so that they
may take hold of the life that really is life."
Life that really is life—that is what I want for
N. One foundation of that life is schooling,
but even more important is the ability to love,
believe, and hope. At this graduation may N
have the grace of these virtues and the
strength to share them. And, thank you, God
for this important passage into the future.

If I Didn't Laugh, I'd Cry

Call to Presence

Creator of the universe, God of compassion,
you are with me at all times.

*(Take a few moments to recall the teenager or
teenagers on whom you wish to focus your prayer.
Recall a recent instance of annoyance with them, a
time when you needed a good sense of humor. How
are you nurturing your sense of humor?)*

Hanging on the Phone and Other Annoyances
Colossians 3:12–13

Living God, sometimes I have no patience when, for example, ℵ hangs on the phone for what seems like forever, and mumbles or shouted expletives are what I hear from the other room. When I am tempted to lose my patience and snap, may I maintain a sense of humor, and remind myself of these words from the Scriptures: "As God's chosen ones, holy and beloved, clothe yourselves with compassion, kindness, humility, meekness, and patience. Bear with one another."

Help me also remember that ℵ is holy and beloved by you. May I learn to bear ℵ with patience, kindness, compassion, humility, and a good sense of humor. But I also need the phone and some peace of mind, so teach me how to be firm and fair. I fail and make mistakes, so it's not fair to expect ℵ to be perfect. Guide me, Holy One, and give me time on the phone.

Don't Wanna Get Up
Mark 7:35

God of all healing, Jesus performed many miraculous cures and told us to heal the sick and suffering. When Jesus told the deaf man's ears to open, "immediately his ears were opened," and the man was cured not only of physical deafness but of spiritual deafness as well.

I know that I am called to heal, but how do I heal N's reluctance to get up and get going in the morning? I need patience and a sense of the ironies of life—humor, in other words. For someone who can stay up all night, chatter away for hours, N seems to have one foot in the grave in the morning. Ah, teenagers!

For those of us who are spiritually deaf, healing God, open our ears. For those, like N, who seem to be physically deaf in the morning, open their ears. Grant that I may hear your invitations to grace even when the invitation comes in the form of an early morning zombie.

ON TEENAGE YELLING
Proverbs 11:17

God, do you get as bent out of shape as I do
by teenage yelling? I honestly don't think N
knows what a conversational tone means.
Unless they're grumbling into their chest,
teens seem to be screaming to people down
the block. It drives me crazy sometimes.

Please, God, let N tone down, and grant
me a sort of mature, calm, good humor about
the whole matter. May I see the sheer energy
of youth in what seems blatant insensitivity.
At the same time, let me correct N just right,
in a style that is as sensitive toward N as I
would like N to be toward me. And always,
may I recall your words,

> Those who are kind reward themselves,
> but the cruel do themselves harm.

With humor may I be kind and give both N
and myself a reward.

INCOMMUNICADO
Matthew 15:11

Holy One, Jesus warned us that "It is not what goes into the mouth that defiles a person, but it is what comes out of the mouth that defiles." But my problem with N is long lapses into sullen silence or maybe cryptic grunts to my openings for conversation. Perhaps N is taking this Gospel warning far too seriously!

Guide me to be considerate, just, and honest, and help me to deal with N's distant and silent ways with a brave heart and blithe spirit. I need to be attentive without giving in to my fears and resentments. In all honesty, though, my God, I would appreciate some conversation beyond monosyllables. Help me to particularly talk to N about ⸺.

BORING, BORING, BORING
Luke 4:18–19

Like many teenagers, $\mathcal{N}$ seems to be bored all the time. Of course anything I suggest is dumb, but $\mathcal{N}$ still looks to me for bright ideas. I'm not totally sure where this boredom comes from, God of surprises, but help $\mathcal{N}$ learn to be inventive, creative, and curious. And grant me the grace to be a person of wonder, curiosity, humor, imagination, and action—a model to $\mathcal{N}$.

Jesus certainly was not bored:

"The Spirit of the Lord is upon me
because he has anointed me
to bring good news to the poor.
He has sent me to proclaim release to the captives
and recovery of sight to the blind,
to let the oppressed go free,
to proclaim the year of the Lord's favor."

Lead $\mathcal{N}$ and me to join in on Jesus' excitement about his mission. Help us to be good news; release us from our lack of vision; free us from our self-imposed boredom. Come, Jesus, send forth your Spirit.

I'm Ugly, I'm Dumb
Ephesians 2:10

Creator God, you didn't make us ugly or dumb, no matter what we look like or what our IQ is. Instead, you said, "We are God's work of art, created in Christ Jesus for the good works which God has already designated to make up our way of life." I pray now that N can see that the whole human family is a work of art chosen by you to do good works.

So many elements in our culture tell us that we are too fat or too thin, too this or too that. Teenagers are particularly vulnerable to the cruelty of snide remarks and cutting words, to the seduction of advertisements and trends. Help N and all teens to see themselves as your works of art, and to love, respect, honor, and appreciate the persons they are. Help me help them, God of all goodness.

STRESSED OUT
Philippians 4:6–7

Holy One, here are words that $\aleph$ and I
need to take to heart: "Do not worry about
anything, but in everything by prayer and
supplication with thanksgiving let your
requests be made known to God. And the
peace of God, which surpasses all understanding, will guard your hearts and your
minds in Christ Jesus."

Stress sometimes takes a terrible toll on
$\aleph$ God, help us both put our trust in you so
that we can cope with the pressures. Help us
figure out which approach to take: to get out
of the situation that causes stress, to change
the situation, or to change our attitude about
the situation. I find working through these
choices hard enough, so guide me. Particularly guide $\aleph$ in dealing with this stressful
situation ⌒. This is my prayer of supplication. Thank you for listening. Send us
peace.

What Am I Going to Do?
Matthew 6:33–34

Teenagers are faced with tough choices—
adult choices—each day, every day. They
have to deal with money, mobility, and
pressures of many kinds. They are pushed
and pulled in opposite directions. God, help
Ν make good choices. May Ν use your
words as a guide when you said to set our
heart on God's "kingdom . . . and [God's]
righteousness. . . . Do not worry about
tomorrow, for tomorrow will brings worries
of its own. Today's trouble is enough for
today."

I need to keep these words in mind, too.
May I model these words for Ν, keeping my
attention on what builds your Reign, your
goodness, today. Guide me to help Ν with
all the tough choices, but especially this one
⌒. Send your light and wisdom, loving
God.

I'm a Failure
Matthew 28:20

Compassionate God, you and I know that
there is a big difference between saying, "I
failed at this or that" and, "I am a failure."
Sadly, a lot of teens don't see the difference.
I make this mistake myself. Surely we fail
sometimes, but we are not failures, at least in
your eyes.

When N is down about failing at
something, let me know what to say so that I
might raise N's spirits above the feeling of
being a failure. Let us remember the example
of Jesus. The majority of people certainly saw
him as the worst sort of failure: a criminal,
crucified, subjected to the most horrible of
deaths. But he conquered death and rose. His
last earthly words were, "I am with you
always, to the end of the age." Help both of
us remember these words and remember the
sustaining presence of Christ. Then we may
rise above our failure and laugh in its face.

STICKING TO IT
Romans 5:3–5

Perseverance is a hard lesson to learn. Teens have so many options today that it's easy for them to give up on challenges and turn their attention to something new and easier. But God, we know that many goals in life are reached only through perseverance.

When I am tempted to counsel $\mathcal{N}$ to take an easier route, remind me of Paul's words: "Suffering produces endurance, and endurance produces character, and character produces hope, and hope does not disappoint us." I do not want $\mathcal{N}$ to suffer, but I also want $\mathcal{N}$ to develop a strong, hopeful character. Sometimes that means making hard choices, holding fast to challenges, and sticking with difficult tasks. Right now, I pray that $\mathcal{N}$ will persevere with the challenge of ⌒. May I guide $\mathcal{N}$ with gentle firmness and sensitive humor.

Friends
and Enemies

Call to Presence

Holy Friend, you always come to comfort and
to invite. You are with me now as I pray.

*(Take a few moments to recall the teenager or
teenagers on whom you wish to focus your prayer.
Who are their friends and enemies right now?
How have you been communicating together
about these friends and foes?)*

FAITHFUL FRIENDS
Sirach 6:14–15

> Faithful friends are a sturdy shelter;
>> whoever finds one has found a
>>> treasure.
> Faithful friends are beyond price;
>> no amount can balance their worth.

Holy Friend, thank you for my friends. Bless each one. They are your gift to me. May I always be a good friend in return.

Now I ask you to bless ℵ with faithful, supportive friends, friends who will be with ℵ not only in the good times but in the bad times as well. May these friends be honest and true. In return, may ℵ learn to be a good friend. God, you know how important our friends are during the teen years. Bless ℵ with these sturdy shelters, these priceless treasures, these faithful friends.

MUTUALITY
2 Corinthians 8:13–14

Faithful Friend, you know that friendship is a kind of dance in which my friend and I share mutually. May Ɲ learn this kind of mutuality in friendship, the kind that Paul talked about when he said, "It is a question of a fair balance between your present abundance and their need, so that their abundance may be for your need," and vice versa.

This kind of mutuality has to be learned, sometimes the hard way. Even so, friends like this play such an important role in enriching life that I can only pray to you, my God, for these kinds of friends for Ɲ. In turn, may Ɲ be this kind of friend, too. I ask this from you, always faithful Divine Friend.

GRACE, LOVE, COMMUNION
2 Corinthians 13:13

God, your servant Paul often ended his letters to the churches by saying, "The grace of the Lord Jesus Christ, the love of God, and the communion of the Holy Spirit be with all of you."

May I always seek grace, love, and communion with all people, but right now I particularly pray for N. In seeking to love N, may I be a model of friendship and kindness, two important gifts N needs in order to grow into a full human being. In particular, in this situation ⌒ may N keep Paul's words in mind and put them into action. Grace, love, and communion be with this young person now and forever.

United in Love
Colossians 2:2

God of all unity, our mission as Christians
is well summarized in Paul's words to the
Colossians: "I want their hearts to be encour-
aged and united in love, so that they may
have all the riches of assured understanding
and have the knowledge of . . . Christ."

We will never understand Christ without
love for one another. Today I especially bring
the name of N before you. Grant N the
grace to be united with friends and all people
in charity, respect, service, and worship. In
this way they will fulfill the law of Christ.
Encourage and grant N the riches of friendship with other people and with Jesus the
Christ.

Unity of the Spirit
Ephesians 4:1–3

"Lead a life worthy of the calling to which you have been called," Paul reminds us, "with all humility and gentleness, with patience, bearing with one another in love, making every effort to maintain the unity of the Spirit in the bond of peace."

This is the calling to which we are called: unity of the Spirit. No easy task for anyone, maybe especially teenagers, and certainly one that we cannot achieve on our own. So, once again, gracious God, I turn to you. Send your abundant blessings upon N and me so that we are indeed worthy of the calling to which you have called us. May N maintain the unity of the Spirit with ⌒ in particular.

Pleasant Speech, Wise Advice
Sirach 6:5–6

Creator of us all, may I teach N how to be a
friend. May we both learn the lessons in this
passage from the Scriptures:

> Pleasant speech multiplies friends,
>> and a gracious tongue multiplies
>>> courtesies.
> Let those who are friendly with you be
>> many,
>> but let your advisers be one in a
>>> thousand.

Help us understand that pleasant speech
can be learned through conscious effort—and
that it is not always suspect. I worry sometimes that we have lost the desire to be
courteous and pleasant; may this never
happen to me or to N . Lastly, please, God,
may N select advisers cautiously and
recognize that just because someone is
friendly he or she is not necessarily wise. I
need help with all this too, my God. Guide us
both. I pray this with confidence in you.

No Greater Love
John 15:13–15

God of all goodness, Jesus taught us friendship through his acceptance and love of the
Apostles and his other friends like Mary
Magdalene and Martha. He paid the ultimate
price for his friends when he laid down his
life for them, having said, "No one has
greater love than this, to lay down one's life
for one's friends. . . . I have called you
friends."

We do lay down our life for our friends
when we help them even in small ways and
make small sacrifices of time and talent.
Encourage N and me to be willing to show
such great love for our friends by helping in
ways that encourage our friends to grow to
full life. May N develop relationships with
friends who understand this kind of love and
friendship and are willing to make such
sacrifices for N as well.

Embraced As Friends
Matthew 11:19

God, Jesus the Christ embraced all people as
friends, people of all backgrounds and levels
of society. His critics thought he took the idea
of friendship too far, and in fact scorned him
for being a friend of "tax collectors and
sinners." Rather than denying the charge,
Jesus agreed with it and even celebrated it.

Good and loving God, help both N and
me put aside unreasonable fears so that we
may be open to friendships with people who
are different from us and who may not be
cool or popular or beautiful or handsome or
brilliant or athletic. Instead, let us begin
relationships with a willingness to listen,
learn, appreciate, and hope for the best, all
the while realizing that we probably won't be
friends to everyone. Give us hope and
openness, tolerance and patience.

LOVE YOUR ENEMIES
Matthew 5:44–45

God, enemies are tough to pray for, let alone love. Even so, Jesus told us, "Love your enemies and pray for those who persecute you, so that you may be children of your Father in heaven; for he makes his sun rise on the evil and on the good, and sends rain on the righteous and on the unrighteous."

God of all, help ℵ and me follow this command. Especially help me be an example for ℵ of how to love and pray for one's enemies. Maybe we can start with prayer and ease our way to love, but your grace must urge and guide us along the way. In a special way, help ℵ pray and love ⌒, someone perceived as an enemy.

OVERCOME EVIL WITH GOOD
Romans 12:20–21

God, you teach us what is good, but doing
good is seldom easy or simple. The Scriptures
tell us, "If your enemies are hungry, feed
them; if they are thirsty, give them something
to drink. . . . Do not be overcome by evil,
but overcome evil with good." God, this is
tough.

In my heart I know that doing good for
those who have done me wrong is the only
road to peace, justice, and harmony in the
world. Without your grace, neither N nor I
can overcome evil in this way. Send your
grace, your Spirit, to us both, so that we can
overcome dislike, anger, and prejudices, and
be open to taking those actions that overcome
evil with good.

A Time to Praise and Thank

Call to Presence

God of all gifts, in praise and thanks I acknowledge your loving presence.

(Take a few moments to recall the teenager or teenagers on whom you wish to focus your prayer. Recollect recent causes for thanks and praise about them. What have you done to celebrate?)

Today I Praise You
Psalm 89:1–6

I join the psalmist to give you praise, God,
our hope:

> I will sing the wonders of your love
> > forever, Yahweh;
> > > I will proclaim your faithfulness to all
> > > generations.
> I will declare that your love is steadfast,
> > your faithfulness fixed as the
> > > heavens.
> The heavens praise your wonders,
> > Yahweh,
> > > and the assembly of the holy ones
> > > exalts your faithfulness.

You do love us, faithful God. You show
your mercy and kindness to us in both
dramatic and quiet ways. I offer you praise
and thanks from a grateful heart. Today I
praise you on behalf of N because of ⌒ .
Indeed, your love is firm and wonderful.

ABUNDANT BLESSINGS
Psalm 104:1–2,24

All creation praises you, living and true God.
In light of your abundant blessings on N
and me, I declare:

> Bless Yahweh, O my soul.
> How great you are, Yahweh, my God!
> You are clothed in majesty and splendor,
>   wrapped in a robe of light! . . .
> Yahweh, how many are the works you
>   have created,
>   arranging everything in wisdom!

I praise you for the gift of teenagers, and
thank you for N's presence in my life.
Thank you for both the times of joy and the
times of challenge; they stretch me to love
and to be wise. Thanks be to you, God of
endless glory.

Do Not Quench the Spirit
1 Thessalonians 5:16–19

In your holy presence, God, I offer you praise
and thanks. As the Scriptures tell us: "Rejoice
always, pray without ceasing, give thanks in
all circumstances; for this is the will of God
in Christ Jesus for you. Do not quench the
Spirit."

And so, Holy One, I do rejoice and thank
you for N and for all the hopes and fears,
frustrations and successes that come with
sharing life with a teenager. May I never stifle
N's spirit, but nourish it and help it grow.
Send your Spirit to flood our soul with light
and hope and love. Praise and thanks to you,
God of glory.

SHOUT FOR JOY
Psalm 100

Holy One, I return to you these words of
thanks and praise:

> Shout for joy to God,
> all the lands!
> Serve God with gladness!
> Come into God's presence with joyful
>   singing! . . .
> We belong to God;
> we are God's people and the sheep of
>   God's pasture.
> Enter God's gates with thanksgiving
> and the courts with praise!
> Give thanks to God; bless God's name!
> For Yahweh is good;
> God's steadfast love endures forever,
> and God's faithfulness to all generations.

I am especially thankful for N and in
particular for these things: ⌣. Grant that
I may let N know of my love and concern,
my hopefulness and gratitude. Bless N, my
good and gracious God.

GRATEFUL SHEPHERD
Luke 2:20

Saving God, you led the shepherds to the humble birthplace of Jesus. In faith, they recognized their Savior. As the Scriptures say, they "returned, glorifying and praising God for all they had heard and seen."

In your name I bless and thank you with a joyful heart, God who loves us. May I always remember that $\aleph$ is your child, your work of art, a temple of your Spirit. Then I will glorify and praise you as I should. As an adult, I too am a shepherd of the young. Teach me to be a wise, careful, grateful shepherd. All honor and praise to you, creator of the universe.

GOD'S LOVE IS EVERLASTING
Psalm 136:1–4,24–25

We give thanks to you, Yahweh, for you
are good.
Your love is everlasting!
We give thanks to you, God of gods.
Your love is everlasting!
You alone do great wonders.
Your love is everlasting!
Your wisdom made the heavens.
Your love is everlasting! . . .
You provide for all living creatures.
Your love is everlasting!
Give thanks to the God of Heaven,
for God's love is everlasting!

You sent $\aleph$ into my care,
Your love is everlasting!
You give me the grace to lead and guide,
Your love is everlasting!

You Are a Blessing to Me
Philippians 1:3–11

God, I thank you for the support and example
of holy people who have guided and blessed
me. I pray with Paul for N, who is a blessing to me: "I thank my God every time I remember you, . . . because of your sharing in
the gospel. . . . And this is my prayer, that
your love may overflow more and more . . .
so that in the day of Christ you may be pure
and blameless, having produced the harvest
of righteousness that comes through Jesus
Christ for the glory and praise of God."

I thank you, God, whenever I remember
N and the part N plays in my life. N calls
me to prayer, to charity, to forgiveness, and
ultimately to holiness. May N love to overflowing, and so may I. May we both give
praise and thanks to you by our overflowing
love for each other and by our good life. This
is our prayer to you, our God.

PRAISE GOD
Psalm 148:1–3,11–13

Praise God from the heavens;
  praise God in the heights;
  praise God, all you angels;
  praise God, all you heavenly hosts.
Praise God, sun and moon;
  praise God, all you shining stars. . . .
Let the rulers of the earth and all peoples
  and all the judges of the earth—
  young men too, and maidens,
  old women and men—
  praise the name of God
  whose name alone is exalted . . .
  and who has raised the fortunes of
   the people.

Praise you, God, for young hearts that are
  searching.
Praise you, Creator, for ℵ in particular.
Praise you, Jesus, for teaching us love.
Praise you, Holy Spirit, for your constant
  graceful presence.
Praise is our prayer to you, God of the
  universe!

BE THANKFUL
Colossians 3:15–16

God, when I despair of teenagers, even Ɲ,
remind me of Paul's words: "Be thankful. Let
the word of Christ dwell in you richly; teach
and admonish one another in all wisdom; and
with gratitude in your hearts sing psalms,
hymns, and spiritual songs to God."

Young people are a source of wonder.
They are new life coming into being, sometimes quickly, sometimes slowly, often
awkwardly, seldom easily. Even when they
sorely disappoint me, let me see past the
problems and rejoice. Even when they mess
up, let me offer them wisdom. And always,
let me give thanks for them. I sing and praise
you, God, Creator, Divine Lover.

A JOYFUL SOUND
Psalm 66:1–8

> Make a joyful sound to God,
>> all the earth.
> Sing the glory of God's name;
>> give glorious praise!
> Say to God, "How tremendous are your
>> deeds!" . . .
> Come and see what God has done:
>> tremendous are God's deeds. . . .
> Bless our God, O peoples;
>> let the sound of God's praise be
>> heard.

You created N to be a blessing to all.
You gave N skills and talents, ideas and
  energy
to offer the human family.
Bless you, God of the universe,
  and thank you for N.
Amen. Alleluia.

Acknowledgments *(continued)*

The psalms in this book are from *Psalms Anew: In Inclusive Language,* compiled by Nancy Schreck and Maureen Leach (Winona, MN: Saint Mary's Press, 1986). Copyright © 1986 by Saint Mary's Press. All rights reserved.

The scriptural quotations cited as "adapted from" are adaptations and are not to be interpreted or used as official translations of the Scriptures.

The scriptural quote on page 61 is from the New American Bible with revised Psalms and revised New Testament. Copyright © 1991, 1986, and 1970 by the Confraternity of Christian Doctrine, 3211 Fourth Street NE, Washington, DC 20017. All rights reserved.

The scriptural quotation on page 123 is from the New Jerusalem Bible. Copyright © 1985 by Darton, Longman and Todd, London, and Doubleday, a division of Bantam Doubleday Dell Publishing Group, New York. All rights reserved.

The remaining scriptural passages herein are from the New Revised Standard Version of the Bible. Copyright © 1989 by the Division of Christian Education of the National Council of the Churches of Christ in the United States of America. All rights reserved.

The text of this book is set in Palatino, a font created in 1948 by Hermann Zapf. The display font, Present, was designed by Friedrich Sallwey in 1974. Typeset by Fine Print Typesetting and Design of Houston, Minnesota.

Genuine recycled paper with 10% post-consumer waste. Printed with soy-based ink.

Give your teen the gift of story.

I Know Things Now
Stories by Teenagers 1
Edited by Carl Koch
Young people write stories about their most
memorable experience of good coming out of a
bad situation, or kindness amid ugliness, or hope
in darkness, or growth amid difficulty.
ISBN 0-88498-384-7
128 pages including 11 student artworks, paper,
$6.95

Friends
Stories by Teenagers 2
Edited by Carl Koch
Teenagers in the United States, Ireland, England,
Canada, and Australia write stories about friends
and friendship.
ISBN 0-88489-492-4
128 pages including 11 student artworks, paper,
$6.95

Finding Hope
Stories by Teenagers 3
Edited by Carl Koch
Teens share their stories of where they find hope
and inspiration.
ISBN 0-88489-524-6
136 pages including 11 student artworks, paper,
$7.95

Every Step of the Way
Stories by Teenagers 4
Edited by Michael Wilt
Young people write about experiences in which they recognize the presence or absence of God in their life.
ISBN 0-88489-581-5
136 pages including 11 student artworks, paper, $6.95

Mountains of the Moon
Stories About Social Justice
Edited by Stephanie Weller Hanson
Ten short stories put flesh and blood on issues of justice.
ISBN 0-88489-542-4
144 pages, paper, $6.95

Waking Up Bees
Stories of Living Life's Questions
Jerry Daoust
Ten short stories vividly portray characters wrestling with important life issues—love, work, money, suffering, communication, vocation, and more.
ISBN 0-88489-527-0
168 pages, paper, $6.95

Available at your local bookstore or phone **Saint Mary's Press** at 800-533-8095; fax 800-344-9225.